For Sawyer.
My brilliant
and bright and
beautiful son.
S.Q.

For my
Friend Paul.
T.H.

CATERPILLAR BOOKS
An imprint of the Little Tiger Group
www.littletiger.co.uk
1 Coda Studios, 189 Munster Road, London SW6 6AW
Imported into the EEA by Penguin Random House Ireland,
Morrison Chambers, 32 Nassau Street, Dublin D02 YH68
First published in Great Britain 2021 • This edition published 2022
Text copyright © Sasha Quinton 2021
Illustrations by Thomas Hegbrook
Illustrations copyright © Caterpillar Books Ltd 2021
A CIP catalogue record for this book is
available from the British Library
All rights reserved • Printed in China
ISBN: 978-1-83891-468-4
CPB/1800/2136/0422
10 9 8 7 6 5 4 3 2 1

The Forest Stewardship Council® (FSC®) is an international, non-governmental organisation dedicated to promoting responsible management of the world's forests. FSC operates a system of forest certification and product labelling that allows consumers to identify wood and wood-based products from well-managed forests and other controlled sources.

For more information about the FSC, please visit their website at www.fsc.org

THE WIND MAY BLOW

Sasha Quinton · Thomas Hegbrook

LITTLE TIGER
LONDON

On the day you were born

the sun rose

brilliant
and bright
and beautiful,

the wild wind may blow you low.

You may fight to

know that...

you are strong enough.

you are smart enough.

you have all you need

And in the morning
the sun
will
rise again

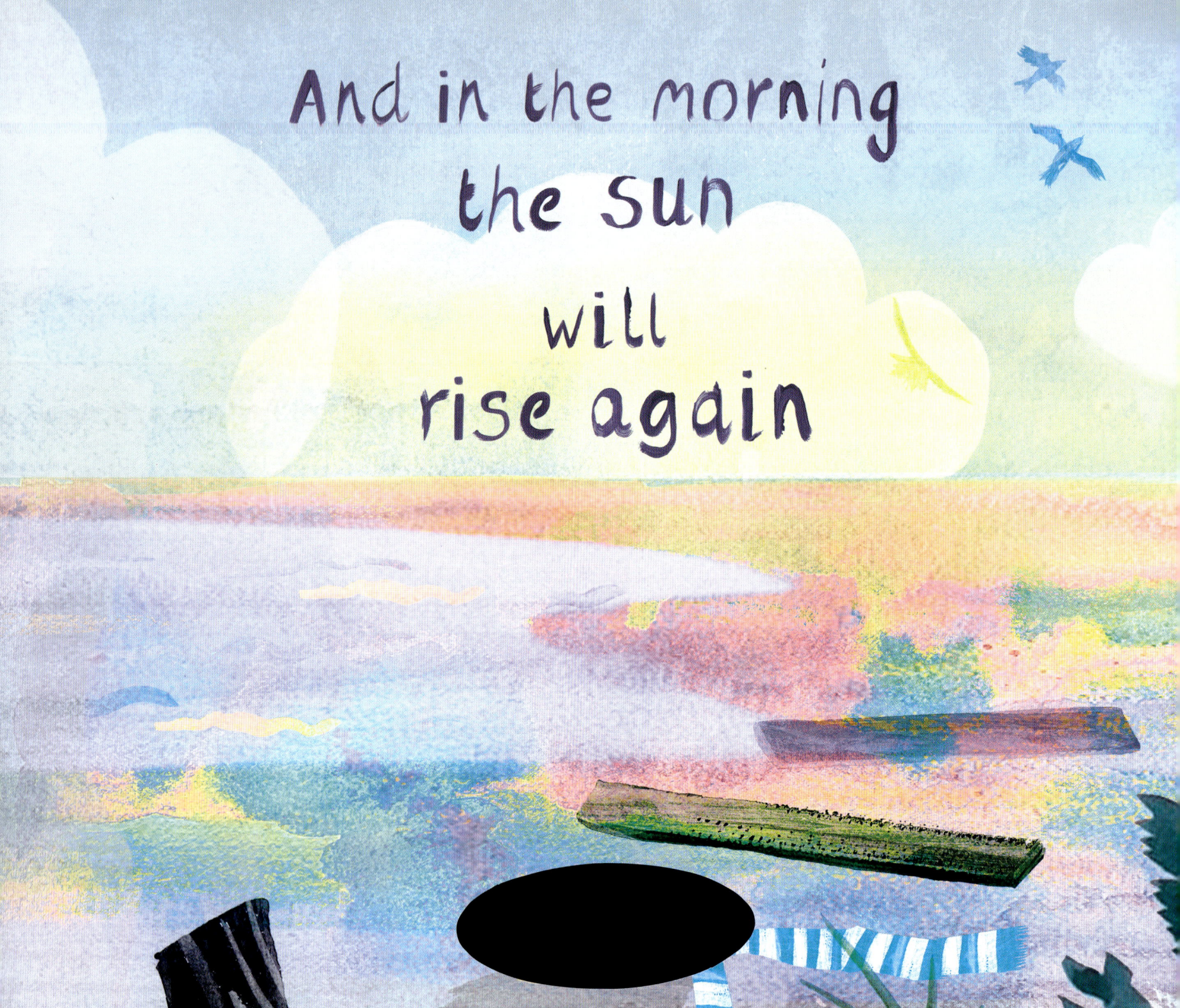